Sticker Scenes

ART COLORING BOOK

Harry Potter

AND THE CHAMBER OF SECRETS™

With Stickers

WORLDWIDE PUBLISHING

SCHOLASTIC INC.

New York Toronto London Auckland Sydney
Mexico City New Delhi Hong Kong Buenos Aires

Copyright © 2002 Warner Bros. HARRY POTTER,
characters, names and related indicia are trademarks
of and © Warner Bros.
WB SHIELD: TM & © Warner Bros.
(s02)
Harry Potter Publishing Rights © J.K. Rowling.
www.harrypotter.com

All rights reserved. Published by Scholastic Inc.
SCHOLASTIC and associated logos are trademarks
and/or registered trademarks of Scholastic Inc.

ISBN 0-439-42526-3

12 11 10 9 8 7 6 5 4 3 2 1   2 3 4 5 6 7/0

Book design by Joan Moloney
Illustrations by Josep Miralles and Ted Enik

Printed in the U.S.A.

First printing, October 2002

Leeches

GILDEROY LOCKHART'S
GUIDE TO HOUSEHOLD PESTS